The Power of Saying "F*** It"

The Power of Saying F*** It

Published by Acushla Publishing

Acushla Publishing
Bath, England

ISBN-13: 978-1493523634
ISBN-10: 1493523635

The Power of Saying "F*** It"

Anne Hassett

CONTENTS

Anne Hassett

Author's Note

In keeping with the whole ethos of the book, I feel it should be short. A long boring tome would defeat the whole idea of ease and simplicity.

CHAPTER ONE

The Defining Moment

For over twenty years, I 'worked on myself '. Great stuff! I made some progress, sure, but still I felt that there was something I was missing. I just wasn't quite getting 'it'.

I am one of those people who believes in being the best; having the best. I don't believe in half measures. Deep inside me I have always believed that we humans are meant to have a good life. I was sure that our Creator hadn't intended all the misery we experience here on Earth and I thought that if only I could remove the layers of self-imposed or society-imposed negativity, then life would be Heaven on Earth.

I was sure that there was some secret; some recipe for success. I felt close to it many times but felt that there was something cloaking it; hiding it from me. That something was, I thought, my programming; the layers of negativity I had accrued in my life so far. Get that off and Bingo! I'd be there. As I work with people and love to help them, I thought if I could crack it, then I could pass on my knowledge to others and we'd all be in clover. But I wasn't really getting anywhere; just going 'round and 'round in circles.

The Dog Chasing its Tail
I have had myself hypnotised, re-birthed, psychoanalysed and regressed to past lives. I have had holographic repatterning, bio-dynamics and the human design programme. I've been on the Chi machine, the Q.X.C.I (Quantum Xxroid Consciousness Interface) machine, not to mention having my astrological chart scrutinised and my tarot cards read. I have drifted into altered states of consciousness in floatation tanks and had deep tissue massage, Thai massage, shiatsu, reflexology, Indian head massage, aromatherapy and lots of other body work, the names of which treatments I have long forgotten.

No one could ever accuse me of not doing some dedicated work on myself! I have done the usual thing of looking at my childhood and my relationship with my parents. I learned to love my Inner Child. I have 'got in touch with my anger' and belted the living daylights out of pillows to release my subconscious and hidden blocks and frustrations. I have had one-on-one counselling and cried many bitter tears. For many years, I put the blame for all my inadequacies, fair and square, on my mother's shoulders, until one helpful therapist sorted me out on that score.

Every now and again, someone would tell me of some wonderful new theory, new therapy, new discovery or the latest and greatest transformational tool and off I would go again, to spend my hard earned money on yet another 'fix'.
I won't say that all these things didn't help. They did. They were hugely helpful. Each new method helped to

remove another layer and to embed in my mind my earnestness about getting myself sorted out, but I felt there was still a missing link. I have been on endless workshops to remove my 'shadow side'. I have been pummelled and poked and detoxed on every level by a variety of dedicated and well-meaning therapists.

Getting in touch with my Inner Child was interesting. I wrote endless letters of forgiveness to my mother, my father, my ex-husband and even myself. I did rituals of burning these letters in the garden. God knows what the neighbours made of it all, as I lit yet another fire! Therapists told me to scream out my pent up anger and frustration and
'to unblock my throat chakra'! The primal screaming presented a bit of a problem: where can you go and scream away all your frustrations in a built-up area, without someone calling the police?

Oh Boy! How I grovelled and gnashed my teeth while re-experiencing all my old pain. How daft can one be? Surely it was enough to have suffered it once without visiting it all again? But no, these therapies insisted that I really 'get in touch' with the pain. 'Get it out,' the therapists said. 'Don't keep it all bottled up inside. Feel the pain.' I laugh now when I remember the times I rolled around on the therapist's floor or on the carpet in my living room, churning up all those old, real or imaginary, hurts. Was I mad or what?

Mad I probably was. Surely, it is insane to put oneself through pain again and again. Wouldn't once be enough? Why go back and revisit and experience it all again?

Dreaming the Impossible Dream?
And what was I hoping to achieve at the end of it all? The perfect relationship? The ideal career? Loads of money? Yes! All of these! The School of 'You can have it all' promised me all those things; all that was in the way were my 'blocks'. Talk about making me feel even more guilty and inadequate. Here I was, trying all this and getting nowhere - not good for the self-worth! But to give me my due, I kept on trying. 'Keep on keeping on' became my motto. One day I would find the therapy, or the workshop, or the book that would turn the key and then, Hey Presto! There would be the golden future of love, prosperity and abundance.

Through those years, I have filled many journals with my pain and my thoughts and have written my hopes and my goals. I have kept endless dream journals. I have looked at myself in the mirror and said my affirmations out-loud and stuck up Post-it notes all over the house to remind me of my goals and my affirmations. (All good stuff really, but not enough.) I listened to subliminal tapes, as I drifted off to sleep and even made self-hypnosis tapes for myself with my voice speaking to me. No one could ever accuse me of not trying. But I was TRYING TOO HARD. And maybe my pattern of struggle started with the school reports which said 'could do better, not trying hard enough'. I couldn't get away from EFFORT. The idea of effortlessness hadn't entered my awareness.

Every now and again, I would hear from friends of a new workshop and they would enthuse about the fabulous results so-and-so had achieved from all this and off I would go again, with my hard-earned cash in my fist. Oh, yes, all those workshop leaders and motivational speakers were genuine and well-meaning people. And, for a while, I would gain some ground until life and I slipped back into old patterns once again. There is no doubt whatsoever that I did make some great strides in those years, but I didn't, somehow, find myself getting to where I wanted to be...

Which was where?

A life of abundance, love, good health and peace - that's where. Because deep down, I believe that is our birthright!

Then, last year, as I was on yet another programme of some kind, going round in circles once again and getting more and more frustrated with myself, I woke up one morning and said...

'F**K IT!'
In that 'F**k It!' moment, I decided to give up working on myself and let things be. It was a 'handing over' moment: a second where I decided to get out of the driving seat. The thought hit me that my ego working on my ego was like a dog chasing its tail.

It was a long awaited moment of realisation: a milestone in my life.

But the best was yet to come, as from that one moment - that flash of awakening - my life has changed in the most wonderful positive ways. In fact, all the things I was desperately striving for have now arrived with ease and joy. Effortlessness has replaced effort.

I don't really think that the years of 'working on myself 'were wasted, they have given me a great understanding of myself and others. And maybe the groundwork was established through all of that for my 'F**k It!' moment! But most of that hard work was really not doing the trick. And I now realise that the bulk of that hard graft was not necessary. It was joyless and punitive.

Looking back to that moment last year, it was a defining moment.

You might not like the vocabulary of that 'F**k It!' moment, but it is an attitude rather than a word. And, hey, these days that word is less objectionable than it used to be. In Ireland, they say 'feck' but somehow it doesn't have the same punch to it. The F**k word has a certain 'Pow' to it. Remember it's only a word, a sound. Even with words, fashions change. There was a huge outcry when George Bernard Shaw used the word 'bloody' in *Pygmalion* and there was shock and horror when Rhett Butler uttered the word 'damn' in *Gone with the Wind*. Thankfully, the F**k word still has a touch of unacceptability about it; if it hadn't, we wouldn't get the same emotional release from using it, nor would it have quite the impact. There is something soo-o-o satisfying in saying 'F**k It!' to mark a shift in attitude or to release some pent up frustration. It is the context in which it is used that is important. And my context was a real letting go; a mega surrender. I got out of my ego and surrendered to something greater than myself. So, what is that 'something'? Actually, it's me, but not me. Let me share a few thoughts with you...

Ego and Higher Self

There are many explanations for the different levels of the human psyche. Freud and Jung had their own labels; the Egyptians had names for the many and different aspects of the human being; there is much documented information about the knowledge of the ancient Hawaiian Kahuna priests, who had a remarkable understanding of the different aspects of each individual. One can look in all sorts of disciplines and belief systems and find that, basically, we are not just the person we think we are but that there are many layers to us. In this book, in the interest of keeping things simple, I will use the phrases Ego and Higher Self.

Ego

The Ego is that little part of us that we generally believe we are. It is the everyday self with all its labels, its beliefs, its opinions, its hang-ups and its pride. It is the part of us that we usually refer to when we talk about ourselves. It is like a made up story of who and what we think we are. It is the persona we put on and wear in the world.

We can say that we are a man, a woman, old, young; we might be Irish or American. We could label ourselves as a doctor, a tradesman, a nurse or a bus driver, depending on our job. We might say we are European, Afro-American, Chinese or whatever. We can be fat or thin, glamorous or plain, clever or average. We could describe ourselves as a mother, father, son or daughter. The list goes on ad infinitum. Think about yourself for a minute. Describe yourself. Add on your political persuasions if you like, or your religious tradition. That is the story of you. Yet, none of it is who you really are. Take away all those descriptions of yourself, pare yourself down to the 'bare bones'; what's left when you take away your story is the Real You: The YOU who observes the other you: The One who watches and listens. I sometimes refer to that watcher part of me as the 'Witness Self'. It is the Higher Self. And, like in Laurel and Hardy, my Witness Self/Higher Self often has a good laugh when it says to my ego 'That's another fine mess you've got me into!' It is good to see the funny side of it and not to take the ego too seriously. It so loves to be taken seriously. That life story that the ego creates about itself is pure illusion.

In Eastern philosophy, they have always known this and refer to the human condition as Maya, which is the Sanskrit word for illusion. Shakespeare said 'All the world's a stage and all the men and women merely players'. If we can see our ego as an actor, we can get an idea of the truth behind the illusion. A film is such a believable illusion that, while we are in the darkened cinema, we are right in there, feeling the feelings, tensing up as we wait for the outcome or crying at the drama. The actors get so caught up in playing their part that they almost become the character they are playing.

What we mistakenly call 'real' life is just like that - a play. It is not real. As we step back from our own lives, observe and become the Witness Self or Higher Self, we begin to get an idea of the play we are in.

The False Self (Ego)
The ego lives in the linear world of duality. It is limited and because it is limited, it is fearful of the future and conditioned by the past. It seldom lives in the now. It has endless desires and endless doubts. It is full of opinions and will go to any lengths to defend those opinions. It loves to be 'right' at any cost.

Grievances, resentment and victim-hood are all part of the ego's identity. The ego sees itself as wronged (seldom wrong, but wronged). It's all someone else's fault! So begins the ego's cycle of looking back at the past to see where it all went wrong and who was to blame, and so - through the ego - we get stuck in shame and blame and martyrdom. The ego glories in it. It loves the pain and the drama; something else to add to the ego's story of who it thinks it is. It thrives on the endless therapies and self- searching. It is only the ego that needs to search. The Higher Self has no need of that; it knows exactly who it is.

If the ego is not living in the past, it is projecting into the future. Both quantum physicists and mystics tell us that there is no past and there is no future. The only 'real' is NOW. The ego doesn't live in the NOW.

As the ego wallows in the grievances and the blame, we get completely stuck. We are still 'back there' somewhere and the more we focus on all that baggage, the more negativity we attract into our lives. By the Law of Attraction, what we focus on, we get more of and if we focus on the pain, we can only get more of it.

We've all been brainwashed with the old saw 'No pain, no gain'. The major religions, like Christianity and Buddhism, see pain and suffering as the way to Heaven or Nirvana; no wonder we have a huge investment in gaining our way through endless pain. It is NOT necessary. Absolutely not! That is all ego stuff. Why would the Higher Self need to suffer? I read somewhere recently that we will continue to suffer until we realise that we don't need to suffer. I instantly resonated with that, as that is what this book is all about. We don't need to suffer... At all!

As the ego continuously strives for and worries about the future, with all its desires and goals, it is never satisfied because, when the goals are achieved, they do not bring the success or security the ego needs, so it pushes more and more, thus perpetuating the cycle of dissatisfaction, fear and futility.

What's it all About?
So, where are we going with all this? You may ask. What has the 'F**k It!' way got to do with it and what is the answer?

Hang on! We need to get a few things straight first; a bit of background:

To survive, the ego has to maintain its separateness. That is its identity. Therefore, to keep that identity, it has to create a sense of 'otherness'. What is not me, as an ego, has to be 'other'. The ego does this by judging and criticising.
Sometimes egos bunch together as tribes or nations or through rigid religious affiliations to strengthen this sense of 'otherness'. A group of egos with a cause can be quite a dangerous thing. As we look around us we see this everywhere; it manifests in politics, nationalism or religion to the point where a bunch of egos, who think they are right, feel completely justified in killing those they have labelled as wrong.

The ego loves to take up positions and stances. This reinforces and validates its existence. Without stances, positions and labels, the ego has no real identity.

The ego identifies completely with the mind and the body. With its identification with the body, it is never satisfied; 'I'm too fat.' 'I'm too thin.' 'My bum is too big or my boobs/penis too small.' So the ego goes to great lengths to remedy these perceived defects, spending inordinate amounts of energy, time and money on products, regimes or plastic surgery to rectify its image. And still it is never enough. All of this creates huge self-generated angst for the ego ... and massive business for the suppliers of the remedies! Yet, the ego is always on a hiding to nothing; it can never be satisfied.

The ego deceives and confuses us by telling us we are the greatest thing since sliced bread or that we are the most useless person that ever walked the earth. It is a false persona. Not only is it a false persona but an insane one.

The ego is afraid that if it lets go of its ideas about itself, it will cease to exist and that is its biggest fear. At one time, I thought I could kill off my ego, as I had a suspicion that it did not have my highest interests in mind, but that is a dangerous, if not impossible, thing to do. The ego will defend its existence by any means it can and trying to kill it off can cause havoc. It will fight back with all it's got. Trying to kill off the ego definitely belongs to the 'don't try this at home' method of self-development!

What a not-so-merry dance of angst the ego leads us in?
No wonder I say 'F**k It!'

So… what to do instead? That's where the Higher Self comes in.

Higher Self
Finding, remembering (re-MEMBERING) and recognising (re-COGNISING) who we truly are at the deepest level of our Being is the only path to lasting happiness.

Whoever Jesus was, he was a great metaphysician and psychologist and exhibited an extraordinary understanding of the human psyche. He taught insights which are even more valid today than they were two thousand years ago. And, by the way, he never said that he was God, only in the sense that we are all God or Children of God. He said 'Know ye not that ye are gods and sons of the Most High.' Buddha and other great teachers espoused and taught similar philosophies.

Jesus said 'Seek ye first the kingdom of Heaven and all these things shall be added unto you.' He then went on to say, 'The Kingdom of Heaven is within.' The Higher Self is within.

The Higher Self is the part of us that is eternal. It is outside of time and space. It exists in the world of non-duality. It is a part of ourselves not encouraged by Western society or Western education. It is the Witness Self. Who is it that observes oneself thinking? Some may refer to it as the Super-Conscious or even the Spirit. It is not the thinking mind, though it observes the thinking mind. It is connected to everything and because it is connected to everything, it knows everything. It is the source of our deepest insights.

The Higher Self is the dwelling place of love, strength, abundance, health, and peace... in fact, of all good things. The Higher Self sees that so-called 'problems' are really only learning experiences. One of the easiest ways to get rid of a problem is to ask oneself 'What is the lesson in this?' Having identified the lesson, the problem very often disappears. The problem is only there to highlight the adjustment that needs to be made.

It is not always easy for us to consciously connect to this part of ourselves, though we are unconsciously connected to it all the time, if we were not we would not exist. This is the 'God bit' of us. Descartes said 'I think, therefore I am.' It should really be 'I am, therefore I think.' If, for whatever reason, you find the word 'God' difficult to come to terms with, think of that pool of energy that Jung referred to as The Collective Consciousness and Einstein called The Unified Field. The Higher Self is an individualised part of that; a spark of the Divine; a fragment of Source. It is a wave in the ocean of consciousness.

I have clients of all persuasions: Christian, Jewish, Buddhist, and Muslim etc. I once had, as clients, some lovely ladies who told me that they were Parsees. In my ignorance, I had to later look it up in the dictionary! There are many paths and many traditions. Therefore, as not to offend my clients of many beliefs, I refer to God/Allah/All-
That-Is as SOURCE. This seems to fit all and offend none.

Who? What? How?
My simplistic way of describing the God and Higher Self bit to myself, so that I can get some understanding of it is...

Before time began there was Source: just Source, nothing else. Source of itself could not know itself, so it decided to expand, to create other bits of itself, so we had Genesis/the Big Bang/the out-breathing of Brahma/Creation. Source sent out zillions and zillions of bits of itself into the void. Some of those 'bits' became galaxies, planets etc. Physicality was created. Some of those 'bits' became us. Originally, we remembered who we were: fragments of Source, made in the image and likeness of our Creator, because after all, we were bits of our Creator.

For eons, we floated about enjoying ourselves, remembering who and what we were. We created things; we had fun. We played with matter and physicality. Then we looked at physicality and decided to explore it in more depth, so in we came. We donned the mantle of physical matter. We immersed ourselves in the physical, but we still remembered who we were. We were still having fun. We created our egos to take charge of the nitty-gritty of our lives, while we (our Higher Selves) could observe the experiment of becoming physical beings. The ego, originally intended to be our servant, developed an inflated notion of its own importance and decided it wanted to become the master. Then, as time went on, we became more and more enamoured of the physical, the ego took more and more control, and we forgot our true identity. There are even some today who think that the physical is all there is! Know anyone like that?

The physical is made up of positive and negative, in the electrical sense; it is a state of duality. Therefore, we have dark and light, up and down, here and there. We ate of the tree of 'good and evil'. This is how our egos began to believe in sickness, death, and limitation of all kinds. We banished ourselves from the Garden of Eden - Our true state.

Time and time again, great Teachers like Buddha and Jesus and Krishna and others who had not forgotten who we were came to remind us - to wake us up from our sleep of immersion in the physical. For a time we got part of their message; we took steps upwards in our evolution. Then our egos or little human selves distorted the message and all kinds of structures and dogmas and institutions grew up around what was intended as a simple message of truth. The message of truth is that we are Divine Beings, unlimited in all things.

We are all a part of Source and our Higher Selves, as fragments of Source, are consciously connected to Source and have access to all that Source is. That means that our Higher Selves are unlimited and eternal. 'Made in the image and likeness of God.'

We talk about 'friends in high places'. Our own Higher Self is the best of all possible friends in the best of all possible high places!

Aha!
As we realise the truth of our being, all falsehood falls away; all limitation dissolves. If we could truly get the message of who and what we really are, our lives would become perfect. If, as it is said, that we are sparks of the Divine or fragments of Source, made in the image and likeness of our Creator, how could we ever be sick, poor, sad or lonely? It would not be possible. If I am Source/God being me and you are Source/God being you, then the truth of who we really are is perfection.

The reality of Source/God is perfection. Source cannot be sick, poor or limited in any way, it is impossible. There is no need to strive. No need for all that effort. The Higher Self takes very good care of us. So, the trick is to remember who we are and to operate ONLY from that reality.

We have been so programmed for millennia that we find it difficult to make that shift of perception; the ego has held sway for so long. But we can 'get it' in the twinkling of an eye when we call the ego's bluff.

That's the 'F**k It!' moment: the moment of surrender and realisation.

'Let go and let God.' Surrender! Override the ego! Shrug your shoulders and say 'F**k It'. Since I did that last year, my life has flowed with ease and comfort and the most amazing things have just come my way. The Higher Self sees the big picture and sends exactly what I need. And, since it is unlimited, what it sends is often much, much better than anything I could ever ask for or imagine when I was operating from ego.

When we operate from our Higher Self (God Self), we are perfect and all around us will reflect that. It is the ego who wants us to keep 'working on ourselves'. The very concept of 'working on ourselves' implies that we are imperfect: flawed - not good enough. That is the ego's strategy to keep itself in control. As we surrender to the Higher Self, the perfection manifests in all areas. So to reach that perfection, the way is to totally surrender. Stop striving.

Allow the Higher Self to be in charge of your life. Don't make a battle between the ego and Higher Self. Just make a decision as to who is going to be in control. Make a decision that the
Higher Self takes up its rightful place as the boss.
Shrug your shoulders to the ego and say 'F**k It!'

I Wouldn't Start From Here
There is a story told of the foreign tourist in Ireland who was asking for directions to Dublin. The Irishman said to him 'If I were you, I wouldn't start from here!' Using the ego as a starting point to get to unlimited abundance, health and happiness is not the way to go.

Therapy has its uses, but it also has its limitations. The ego working on the ego can only go around in circles. Another ego (that of the therapist) working on one's ego is equally limited. The therapist who reminds you of who you truly are and helps you to connect to the deepest level of your being, your Higher Self, has the best chance of success.

Any therapist who tells you that you are 'less than' or 'flawed' can only cause you unnecessary pain and hold back your evolution.

Endlessly going over the hurts and traumas of our past is only perpetuating the pain.

If a child is having a nightmare, you don't try to fix the nightmare, you gently wake the child up.

So it is with reality. Don't try to fix the illusion, but wake up to the truth of who you are.

The greatest and highest form of healing that any of us can do for each other is to keep reminding one another of the true nature of our being. Waking one another up is the ultimate healing and kindness. In fact, it is the ONLY kind of healing; all else prolongs the illusion and separation.

In a Nutshell
Recognise the expressions and levels of your being: ego and Higher Self. The ego is limited and when we operate from ego, we can only be limited. The Higher Self is unlimited and operating from The Higher Self creates unlimited wellbeing, joy, abundance and love.

CHAPTER TWO

Source

God/Allah/Higher Power/Holy Spirit/Brahma/All-That-Is/Awareness/The Universe... fill in the blank!

In the Western world, most of us have come to hate or fear the word 'God'. No wonder, as so much suffering has been inflicted on mankind 'in the name of God'. We have had millions killed horribly in the Inquisition - all 'in the name of God'. Millions of women, over a couple of centuries in North America and Europe, tortured and killed for witchcraft, when all they were, were wise women, medicine women and herbalists of their time; women who had the secrets of the gifts of nature handed down to them by their forebears. And then there were the Crusades with all of the bloodshed and the massacre of thousands of natives in South America by European settlers. The list goes on and it was all done 'in the name of God'. What had God to do with any of it? It was all mankind's doing. Nice to be able to pass the buck, Eh?

No wonder modern, educated people don't want to know! Who would want to be associated with a 'God' who could countenance such atrocities? And

today we have fundamentalist religionists of different persuasions, willing to kill and terrorise because their 'God' tells them to!
Humans have made a God in their own image and likeness and not the other way around.

And now we have also become so scientific that we have rational explanations for everything and some see God as fanciful and belonging to the beliefs of the superstitious and the unenlightened. So, God has gone out of favour as a word anyway. If you are one of those who are comfortable with the word 'God', then fine, but if you are not, then find another word. I suggest 'Source', because there is a Source: A Creator. We can't have got here by chance. The Universe is an intelligent matrix of awareness.

There is no need to have studied quantum physics, or indeed any physics at all, to know that everything in the Universe is energy. If you have studied physics, you will know that, right down there somewhere, at the very basis of it all, energy is either a wave or a particle. The wave and the particle are interchangeable; the particle can become a wave or the wave can become a particle. So all that 'stuff' is really 'non-stuff'. It has no concrete reality at all. The table that appears as solid (and it certainly feels solid if I bang my knee on it), when you look at it from the scientist's point of view, is made up of molecules, which are composed of atoms and then the atom is made up of swirling masses of energy; it is really not solid at all. It feels solid because the mind perceives it as solid. It is, as the Buddhists would say, an imputation of the mind. The mind gets a lot of things wrong.

Shift Gear

If only we could change our perceptions: our belief systems, really, really deep down change them; we could do all sorts of amazing things. It all boils down to how we perceive and believe. Most of our beliefs are of the ego and many of our beliefs are those we have taken on from others, such as parents, religious leaders and teachers. They took those beliefs on board, unquestioningly, from those before them and those before them got them from... you get the idea. Now and again, a wise soul questions things, adjusts perceptions and makes amazing strides and everyone calls him/her a genius. We are all geniuses who haven't yet woken up. All we have to do is to get away from the ego's limited thinking and... Wowie! The Universe reveals its secrets to us. It reveals to us via the Higher Self, which is connected to Source. One of the best things we can do for ourselves is getting out of our mind!

The Buddhists say 'The mind is the slayer of the Real'. The mind is the province of the ego.

So, when we try to understand Source/God with the mind, we haven't a chance in hell. (Or Heaven or anywhere else!) How can a finite mind understand the Infinite? The mind is part of the ego's set of tools and as the ego is limited, so is the mind. There is an aspect of the mind, which some Eastern philosophers call the Higher Mind. This Higher Mind may get some grasp of the nature of the Divine. The Higher Mind operates at levels achieved in meditation or altered states of consciousness. (The ego hates all that stuff!)

But, forget about all that. Trying to figure it all out is not necessary. Just ask yourself; what part of your Essence or your Being makes your heart beat, your lungs breathe, your hair grow, and wounds repair themselves? There is some amazing intelligence operating behind it all somewhere, isn't there?

Yogis, who spend years studying the inner dynamics of Higher Mind, can regulate their own heartbeat. They can even remain in states of suspended animation for lengthy periods of time. But we don't need to look at all that, all we want is a better life, less stress, more success and happiness. Yes? Unless you want to become a Yogi; as a career option, being a Yogi is not a lot of fun; the pay sucks, the uniform is draughty and sartorially questionable and the food is terrible! Becoming a Yogi is not what this book is about. This book is about finding the way to a better life. The 'F**k It!' way works. It has worked for me and, goodness knows, if it can work for me, it can work for anyone!

Get out of Your Own Way
If we can get the ego out of the way and let the Inner Higher Self (the fragment of Source that we are, that keeps our heart beating and our bodily functions working without our conscious thought) be in charge, it will do a wonderful job. All we have to do is get out of the way. Relax! Someone once said 'Wear the world like a loose garment'. Surrender! Hand over! It doesn't

mean that we sit on our butts and vegetate, far from it. It does mean that we get on with our lives and do what we always did and do it with joy. But we surrender the process and the outcome to the Higher Self.

I once knew a guy who used to say 'When you hand your will and your life over to the care of God, the rest of your life is none of your business.' He was someone who had really cracked it!

I now know that, when my life is going pear-shaped, all I have to do is ask myself which part of me is running the show today? If it's all going pear-shaped, it's the ego. So, immediately, I hand over the whole shebang to the Higher Self and in no time at all it gets sorted beautifully. And much better than 'i' (The ego/little me) could ever have
done it!

It is so simple really.

Your sole business in life is to attain God-realisation. All else is useless and worthless.

Sivananda

It is a huge arrogance to think that we are separate from Source. The original meaning of the word sin comes from an archery term, which means to miss the point. The point that we are missing is that we are not separate from Source.
That is the sin, which is so bandied about. When the teachers referred to us as sinners, they were merely pointing out to us that we were missing the point. Our

original sin was when we first decided we were separate beings and we virtually cut ourselves off from any conscious awareness of Source.

'Don't give me all that religious stuff,' I hear you say.

Wait a minute! Don't throw the baby out with the bath water. Religions may have lost the plot, but the teachers of old knew a thing or two. It is really the religions that are sinning. (They miss the point!) Any religion or belief system which tells us that we are 'less than' or that we are separate from Source is to be avoided. There is a big difference between religion and spirituality. Religion is a man-made system and may indeed contain some spirituality, but true spirituality is a 'knowing': a knowing of one's own Divine nature and ones connection to All-That-Is.

All-That-Is is Source. You may call it God, Brahma, Creator, Allah, Awareness. You can call it whatever you like, as the naming of it is only for our own use. Source has no need of names. Indeed, naming it or trying to label it is limiting it. It is beyond all that. It is unfathomable and well beyond our limited understanding. Always, the egotistic mind wants to understand, wants to intellectualise and to put names, categories and labels on everything. The more one gets into the complexities of categorising, naming and trying to explain Source, the more one misses the point. Source is nameless and yet we need some name for it as we talk to one another about it. But no name can describe or define Source, nor get within a whisker of any kind of understanding of it. Our own Higher Self is a fragment of this great and unfathomable Essence. We, each of us, are a wave in the great ocean of Awareness.

Words are of the mind and are thus limited. As we contemplate this truth, of the limitations of words, we begin to get a slight understanding of the fable of the tower of Babel. A certain word may mean one thing to me, another thing to you and something entirely different to someone else. Our perception depends on where we are in our level of development.

Get Out of Your Mind!
One really good way to connect with Source is through meditation.

Don't let the word 'meditation' put you off. The mere mention of the word conjures up pictures of monks or holier-than-thou (Bless 'em!) folks, sitting cross-legged in the lotus position. Leave religion out of it altogether, or leave it in if you wish. Meditation is the stilling of the mind so that the ego, and all its shenanigans, is out of the way and one can reach the Higher Self and, through the Higher Self, Source. Neither do you need 'trappings'; statues, incense, candles, bells or such. If you like them, they will do no harm and may help you to relax. Nor do you have to join the kaftans, beads and sandals brigade. What is going on on the outside is not important, that's ego stuff. The Higher Self is more aware of what is going on on the inside. It's all an inside job! You can meditate in your business suit on the train, or in the office restroom, or anywhere you like when you find the time.

If you are fortunate enough to live in the country or near a park, you will discover that meditating in nature is very beneficial. The vibrations or frequencies of nature can be so uplifting and can lift our vibrations to new heights.

Everything is energy and everything is vibrating at different frequencies. The frequencies of nature have a very beneficial effect and help to enable us to make easier conscious contact with Source.

There is no need, either, to spend hours at it. Just start with fifteen minutes. If you can't do that, try five. And do it more than once a day. Fifteen minutes, twice a day may be all you can cope with at the start, or it may be all you have time for, but as you get in to it and begin to feel the benefits, you'll actually want to do more. It is time well spent and will produce remarkable results in your life.

Now, talking of meditation and doing it are two very different things. The Western mind is not geared for quiet contemplation. And that is what meditation really is: quiet contemplation and a stilling of the mind. It is not easy and, because it is not easy, most people give up after a few tries.

I hear people say 'But my mind keeps wandering.' Yes, it will. But just keep on. The trick is not to hang on to any of the stream of thoughts that pass through the mind. See them swim by like goldfish in a tank. Don't focus on them.

Whatever you do, don't strain. Let the thoughts swim by without hanging on to any of them. Focus on your breathing. Keep bringing your mind back again and again, as it strays off, hanging on to yet another thought. I sometimes feel that my mind is like an untrained monkey, hopping here there and everywhere. But it can be trained. It is well worth persevering. But do this with ease - no force - just keep calmly and steadily bringing the mind back to the breath. Make it joyful; otherwise, what's the point?

Let Go - Get in the Flow!
'So,' you are saying. 'Do I have to meditate to do the 'F**k It!' method of making my life better?' NO. All you have to do for the 'F**k It!' method is Let Go; let go of the ego and let the Higher Self take control. 'Let go and let God'; if you want to phrase it that way.

I have only thrown in the ideas about meditation if you wish to go a bit further; if you wish to have a more conscious contact with your Higher Self. But, whatever you do, don't strain, don't try. Don't make EFFORT. Be effortless. Nature is effortless. Get in the rhythm. Get in the flow. If you let go and let the Higher Self take over, it will all flow to you and it will flow in ways that you could never imagine and in the abundance that you could never imagine. There is no end to our evolution process; we truly are gods in the making. The sky's the limit, literally. And don't you want the best for yourself? The very, very best? The best of all possible growth, development and evolution?

In a Nutshell

When we come to accept that there is an All-Intelligent and Unlimited Power in the Universe, that we are part of and can connect to, we can 'plug in' and download from this unlimited reservoir of all good things. Then life becomes unimaginably wonderful. It is really, very simple.

Anne Hassett

CHAPTER THREE

Live in the Solution and Not in the Problem

Whatever problem you have, let it go. 'F**K It!'

Don't make a friend of your problem. Don't entertain it. Would you have a miserable house-guest to stay in your home? Your psyche is your inner 'home' and problems are miserable house-guests. Turf them out! Don't entertain worry and problems in the house of your thoughts. It was probably the ego that created the problem anyway. If this guest wants to hang around, tell it politely (or not so politely if you like) to clear off. But don't focus on it; don't fight it. Fighting anything only gives it more power. Carl Jung, the famous Austrian psychologist, said 'What you resist, persists'.

Why do we always feel that we have to fight with our problems? How often do we use the expression 'wrestling with a problem'? Do that and it will hang around.

Don't try to root it out. Ignore it! Starve it of attention! If you starve the unwelcome guest, they will soon pack their bags and leave!

Jung's idea that 'what you resist, persists', is based on the idea that whatever you give your attention to, you get more of. Ralph Waldo Trine, in his famous book, *In Tune with the Infinite*, said something to the effect too, when he said 'the optimist is right and the pessimist is right'. The optimist expects everything to go right and so it does. The pessimist expects everything to go wrong and, sure enough, it does.

This is the Law of the Universe: the Law of Attraction. What we focus on we get more of. Henry Ford said 'Whether you think you can or you think you can't, either way you are right'. Shakespeare said 'There is nothing either good or bad, but thinking makes it so'. Jesus put it 'As a man thinks, so he is'. Buddha said 'Energy follows thought'. And the Bhagavad-Gita says 'Man is made by his
belief. As he believes, so he is'.

Affirmations? Yes, but with a New Slant.
When I had my 'F**k It!' insight - my defining moment – I decided to give up all the affirmations. Years of making them had produced a barely perceptible improvement.

But the mind has to have its constant chatter: its inner self talk. It's not possible to shut it up. So, if it has to have all that self-talk, it must be positive. The affirmations I used to make, like 'I am wealthy', would always bring the snide reply from my ego of 'Oh Yeah! What about the bills?', or some such negative response. The affirmation 'I live in an abundant universe' would elicit something like 'Where are the signs of that then?' So, one thought or belief cancelled out the other. So, in my new 'F**k It!' mind-set, where I wasn't as stressed as before, I found a new trick to get one over on the ego. I began to say 'I love wealth' or 'I love the freedom money can buy'. The ego had no answer to that! It couldn't really argue with an established belief and the focus was still on wealth and not the lack of it. It really is amazing that, without changing my diet one little bit, I have lost quite a few pounds in six months just by saying 'I love to be slim'. The focus is then off the weight problem and very much on what I would like instead.

Health problems, thankfully, have never been an issue for me. Somewhere along the way - way back - I unconsciously learned to never give sickness the chance to be a house-guest in the house of my awareness. But if ill-health is your problem (and we all have our own issues to work on); instead of saying 'I am healthy', when you know darn well that you are not (thus setting up an impasse or even a conflict in your mind), trick your negative ego by saying 'I love health', 'I love to be healthy', or 'Being healthy is great'. The ego can't really argue with that and the focus is then on health and not on illness.

The problems you encounter mostly in your life may be to do with unsatisfactory relationships, so use the same system, i.e. 'I love to be in a loving relationship.' Whether you are in one or not at the time, you'd like to be, so the focus is on what you want and not on what you don't want. The Law of Attraction will do the rest. The ego won't have a leg to stand on and your Higher Self can get on with manifesting your desire.

Each of us has our own issue, or issues, to work with. It's as if, before we incarnate, we chose a subject from the Cosmic Curriculum. Getting to grips with our particular choice or challenge brings us closer to achieving Mastery, which is why I believe we are here.

Take a Break
Whatever problem you have or think you have, give yourself a break from it for a day or two by saying 'F**K It!' Letting go! Surrendering! Not giving the problem the time of day. While you are having time off from the problem, the answer will probably appear or the problem will disappear, especially if you have called in the assistance of your Higher Self. Handing the problem over to the Higher Self creates the miracles. 'Let go and let God', as some say. Einstein got a lot of his best ideas in his sleep; that's when the ego is out of the way and the Higher Self is operating.

Sometimes I ask myself what a wise old sage would do in a particular problem situation. That's really turning it over to The Higher Self, because the Higher Self is the wise old sage. You'll get the answer. Live as if you already have the answer.

Of course, the ego loves the problem. Its total identity is its investment in limitation. The ego, being limited, loves to stay limited; loves to keep us limited, and then it can still be the boss. It is still in control.

So, with regard to the problem, 'F**k It!' and leave it. Embrace the answer. If the answer hasn't come yet, it soon will.

Another trick is to see where you are right now. NOW! Not 'these days', but right now: this minute. Are you alive? (You gotta be if you are reading this!) Is it really so bad? Maybe right at this moment you have everything you need but you are worried that it may all be taken away from you, or that you are not going to have enough for the future. The future hasn't come yet. All we ever have is now. Do we even know there is a future? We believe there is because everybody says so. But the only time we ever can be sure of is NOW. And it is the only time in which we can do anything.

Don't regret the past either. You did the best you could at the time. Everyone does. 'Do they?' I hear you say. Of course they do, if they knew how to do it any differently or better, they would have done so.

Get Out of the Driving Seat
Most of us are addicted to control. Control is the flip-side of fear. Fear is what makes people want to control. If they had no fear, they could let go and let things be. If you have a need to be in constant control, then you need to really apply the 'F**k It!' principle. That need to control is an addiction.

There are many types of addictions. Some think that the only addictions are to drugs or alcohol. There are many more: work, sport, religion, unhealthy relationships, sex, in fact anything that gives us a 'fix';

that gives us an escape from our emptiness or pain; our need for an identity; our fear of not being or having enough. Addictions hide from us our inability to have a meaningful relationship or to experience intimacy.

Some of the symptoms of addiction are:
1. Obsessive thoughts about the substance or process we are addicted to; i.e. alcohol, food, exercise etc.
2. Tension in the physical body.
3. The ego says that things must be different in order to enjoy life; 'If only I hadn't done that in the past', or 'I wish things were different in the future, then I could enjoy life'.
4. Seeing life as a problem - instead of a game. 'You struggle and then you die', is most people's mantra. What a lousy way to live! See life as a game. Have fun.
5. Competition. Must win or lose instead of just accepting life as it is.
6. Sense of separation, which has, as its symptoms, fear, anger and resentment instead of Joy, Love and Peace.

I once heard a recovering alcoholic say that until she found recovery and her Higher Power; she felt she had a Godshaped hole in her middle. Jung said 'Addiction is a thirst for spirituality'. Which brings us back to that bit about reconnecting to our Higher Selves!

When operating from the Higher Self, we can be surrounded by drama and still be composed. One then becomes the witness and not the victim. We can sit in the eye of the hurricane, relax and say 'F**k It!' Being right there in the midst of what we perceive as disaster, we can buy in to it, feel victimised, cry 'Ain't it awful', 'Why is this happening to me'? Or we can look at it objectively, withdraw our attention from it by adopting the 'F**k It!' philosophy and just be a witness to it; thus we starve it of energy and life. But, Boy! Doesn't the ego love a bit of drama!

Living in the solution means seeing the positive.

Abraham Lincoln once said that 'most people are as happy as they make their minds up to be'. Happiness is a decision. How we view things is also important. When we stop judging things or events as good or bad - getting out of the 'ain't it awful' frame of mind and seeking the solution - we feel good. And, remember, what we focus on, we get more of.

Give up the worry and angst. Chill out! 'F**k It!'

All Work and No Play
Workaholism should be given a large dose of the 'F**k It!' treatment. Workaholism is an illness, just as are any of the other addictions. In fact, there are now groups of Workaholics Anonymous in many major cities. Workaholics, as they climb the ladder to success, will buy into fear, which in turn makes them competitive and alienates them from others. They will neglect their families and themselves and the important things of life. Their values become distorted and they develop fear, worry and anxiety.

Of course, Workaholism is one of the most difficult of all the 'holisms' to detect, as the work ethic is so admired in our society.

I work in a major Asian banking city from time to time and am always appalled at the life these people live. They work well into the late evening, sometimes six days a week... and for what? Security? They have no quality of life. The place is like one giant labour camp, and that applies to the ex-pats there too. I suspect that most major cities anywhere in the world are much the same. Oh Boy! Our Creator never meant our lives to be like that. It is only fear that motivates and that fear comes from the ego. The Higher Self, as part of Source, can know no fear for it knows that there is plenty to go around and plenty for everyone. But unless one is aware and connected to that Higher Self then fear will hold sway. It is not just in the corporate world that work addiction is endemic; it also affects so many women. These are women who are so addicted to work that they never sit down. They always find something more to do; people to see, calls to make, another closet to clear, already clean surfaces to be wiped, pillows to fluff... and on and on it goes.

WORKAHOLISM CAN KILL. There ought to be a government health warning!

When is enough, enough? On our deathbeds will we wish we had worked more or will we wish we had spent time with family and friends, or seen more of the world or done more for others or taken time to enjoy the sunset and smell the flowers? Skip a few chores. Will it really matter in the end? How much better to give time to a child or to spend quality time with friends and family?

Some of us don't even give time to ourselves; time to get to know ourselves; time to work out who we are and what we really want in life. We are so caught up in the race to get more, usually more 'things', that we lose sight of our Inner Being. We lose sight of the deeper meaning. No wonder there is so much unrest. The unrest in each one of us, as part of the whole, contributes to the unrest of the whole. Mankind has lost the plot!

As we give more time to ourselves, the questions arise; 'Who am I?' 'Why am I here?' 'What is my purpose in life?' As we contemplate these questions and seek the answers, we become more adjusted human beings; we get to work out what is really important and what is not. To what is not important, we can say 'F**k It!' and give time and attention to what is.

We really need to make time for ourselves; time to think; time to enjoy; time to have fun; time for family and friends. And, most importantly, time to nurture ourselves. As we nurture ourselves, we feel more inclined to nurture others. Be good to yourself. When did you last have a massage?
When did you last have a day off that was just for you? You can be absolutely sure that the world will still go on turning even if you are not actively involved in the process!

To make life a bit easier, give up control. Delegate. The ego, in its arrogance, sees only one way of doing anything... the ego's/'my' way! Give up 'shoulds'. An Irish friend of mine says 'Stop shoulding on yourself'.

Relaxed happy people become magnets for all sorts of good things. That doesn't mean that you sit on your butt and do nothing. Do it, whatever it is, but do it in a relaxed but purposeful way. Does a rose struggle to bloom? Get in the rhythm of life, but don't drift. Be like a surfer; let the wave carry you.

Focus on the answer and give no energy to the problem. Let your Higher Self work things out for you. Tell the ego to take a break.

And, as for the problem; 'F**k It!'

In a Nutshell
Don't entertain problems; they make rotten house-guests. Focus on what you want and not on what you don't want. Let go of overwork. Live in the now and trust the Higher Self to provide.

Enjoy life. Be a human 'being' and not a human 'doing'.

CHAPTER FOUR

Break the Silly Rules

Not all the rules, only the silly ones!

Our lives are governed by scores of ridiculous rules. We have to have laws and rules in our society or we would have absolute anarchy and be in a real mess. I'm talking here of some of the silly rules that we just obey without question. On close examination, these silly rules do not enhance our lives. Instead, they keep us in an unquestioned bondage to old - and oft-times outmoded — ideas that have long outlived their usefulness; if they ever had any.

Anyone who ever became great in this world questioned things; they questioned the mindless repetition of behaviour, which is usually carried out 'because everybody does it'. Are we sheep? One would certainly suspect so if one just observed the January Sales, the addiction to certain 'soaps', the weekend activities in suburbia of grass cutting and car washing, 'because everybody does it'. The commuters, who have to sit in the same seat in the same train every day and who feel very discomfited if 'their' seat is occupied by someone else. They are hypnotised by sameness; lulled into a state, which is less than awake. How can anyone be awake or aware when operating like this?

We are brainwashed and conditioned to a point where we don't think for ourselves anymore.

Why not try to walk to work by a different route, or catch a different train or drive on an unfamiliar road. It helps to keep us awake. Dare to do things differently. Step out of the herd. When we stay awake, we see more; we see new opportunities; we are stimulated; inspiration comes. Never be afraid of change, the only thing we can be sure of in life is change; it is all around us in nature. If things did not change, there would be no growth and if something is not growing, it must surely be dying.

The only thing constant is change.
The I Ching

Stop 'Shoulding' on Yourself
An Irish friend of mine once caught me out, as I afflicted yet another 'should' on my- self. When she said 'Stop shoulding on yourself', the humour made a lasting impression and keeps me mindful not to use the 'should' word. Our mindsets are full of 'shoulds', 'ought tos', 'musts' and such like. They limit us. A teacher of mine used to call them SMOG; Should, Must, Ought to, Gotta. Who says these limiting words? Where have they come from? Whenever we are using those words, we are stepping out of our own power and responsibility and giving it away to some vague 'They'. 'They' say we should. 'They' say we ought to. 'They' say we must.

What a great cop-out. Giving our power to that mysterious 'They' helps us to avoid responsibility and greatly limits us. And who is 'They' anyway?

When the shoulds come up, ask yourself what you really want to do; what is best for your own growth and wellbeing? I know that when I do something because I should and not because I want to, then I can hold resentment about it. Do it with good grace or not at all.

There are many good rules that keep our society from falling apart. We all need boundaries and guidelines. The Twelve Steps of Alcoholics Anonymous has been cited as the greatest spiritual movement of the twentieth century. It has certainly saved millions of lives and turned hopeless drunks, who were considered to be the dregs of society, into useful and highly spiritual people. Interestingly, A.A has no rules, only suggestions and guidelines. Children may need rules but, surely, adults could benefit better from guidelines.

Some Silly Rules:
I quote some of, what I see as, silly rules here. I asked my friends for their examples and got a variety of interesting responses. Think of what you might consider to be a ridiculous rule.

Rules like...
1. *Little boys/men don't cry.* Why not? If they did then they would be happier and live longer. Suppressed emotions lead to 'dis-ease'. Generally, women live longer than men. I'm

sure it is because they cry. They know how to let go and let all the anger, hurt and pain out. From an early age, society instils in the male that he mustn't be a sissy; he has to look and act all brave and strong, even if he is screaming with pain inside. In some repressed societies, men are so closed off that the only way that they can offload their pain is by inflicting it on others: by either suppressing their womenfolk or by being overly aggressive. As a result, we have gang warfare or terrorism.

2. ***You have to give everyone you meet, like work colleagues, members of your golf club, the neighbours, the neighbour's dog etc., a Christmas card at Christmas.*** Why? You see them daily or weekly. You could give them a hug (if appropriate) and a smile and actually wish them 'Happy Christmas' there and then and, thus, save loads of man hours shopping for, selecting, buying and writing cards, when you could be doing something far more interesting and productive, not to mention saving resources, paper and trees and not contributing to global warming. By all means, send a card to Auntie Liz in Newport, you don't see her often and it will cheer her up. But you could also send her a card in March, July or October! Or, better still, go and see her and if you can't, phone her.

3. ***You mustn't be on your own at Christmas.*** Like myself, several of my friends are single people, who lead exceptionally busy lives, and they would like nothing better than to have

Christmas Day alone to watch their favourite TV programmes and read the nice book they have bought as a Christmas present from themselves, to themselves. But no, family and friends, who are in couples can't get their heads around this concept. So, my friends have had to lie to avoid spending Christmas with their daughter's husband's hard-of-hearing mother, who has to be shouted at to have any kind of conversation. Then there's the son-in-law's drunken brother, his neurotic wife and the badly behaved kids! And there's Uncle Charlie, who gets drunk, gropes all the women present and bores everyone to death with his unfunny jokes and his tall tales of his past glories and exploits. Who wouldn't rather be at home in front of the fire with a box of naughty chocolates and a favourite book or TV programme?

4. *You mustn't, shouldn't, ought not, talk to the bum in the street.* Why not? He's a human being and 'There but for the grace of God'!
5. *You should save for a rainy day.* If you believe that what you focus on, you will attract, then by saving for a rainy day, you will create a rainy day. Saving for a rainy day comes from fear and poverty consciousness. Splashing out when you feel financially challenged gives out the vibe to the Universe that you believe in abundance and this attitude will attract abundance. Adjust your belief, not the situation.
6. *You must acquire loads of 'stuff'; latest TV, latest sound system, bigger car, boat,*

swimming pool etc. Sure, all these things are nice but the pursuit of them can cause an awful lot of anxiety and suffering. When you say 'F**k It!' to this rat race of acquisition, you will be a lot happier and the 'stuff' may just possibly turn up anyway, as it is your consciousness that will attract prosperity and that is an inside job!

> *Man's only enemy is FEAR.*
> *Florence Scovel-Shinn*

7. **People in business must wear black, grey or navy.** It is supposed to endow them with an air of reliability and respectability. (Does the mafia spring to mind?) Wouldn't it be great if our bankers, lawyers, estate agents or accountants wore bright cheerful colours? It would cheer us all up. For the last few centuries, men have taken to wearing dull and boring colours and their apparel has hardly changed since the Middle Ages. Now, women in business are aping that style and in most cities, at lunchtime, all one sees is an ocean of dark colours. What's wrong with a woman wearing a nice red, blue or green suit to the boardroom? I'm sure that secretly many men, even the most heterosexual, would love to wear the glorious colours and fabrics that the men of the middle ages wore; the sensuous velvets; the shimmering silks and the dazzling jewellery. But they don't have to go quite that far, just brighten up and lighten up. A snazzy tie or even a lighter colour suit would help. After all, it is

usually the male of any species that is noted for its attractive plumage! Colour has an uplifting effect on the brain and can engender creativity; it stimulates productivity. It also promotes good spirits and joyfulness. So, 'F**k it!' Be daring and wear something a little less conservative. Brighten up our lives! And rising morale and good spirits in the workplace might even mean the business is more successful.

8. *You have to know everything (or at least pretend to).* NO! You certainly don't! That's ego at work. The ego thinks that to be seen not knowing everything is a sign of stupidity or weakness and it feels embarrassed. The Higher Self knows everything anyway. The Higher Self's knowing is more wisdom than knowledge and therefore of a higher order. Keep the ego in its place by admitting you don't know the answer if you don't. By admitting one doesn't know everything, it makes one seem more human and less of a threat. No one likes a 'know-all'.

9. *Practise makes perfect.* Not necessarily! If you keep practising something the wrong way, it will never be perfect. All the practise in the world won't make the wrong way right, if you keep on doing it. Be honest with yourself and just change the way you do it.

10. *People shouldn't have office relationships.* If you happen to be lonely and your Higher Self has placed you in this particular company, adjacent to what could be your soul-mate in the next cubicle, then, if you take notice of this

'rule', you could miss out on the opportunity of a lifetime to find happiness and companionship.

11. ***A man should always ask a woman out and never the other way around.*** Why, for goodness sake? In this day and age, surely that silly old rule could be scrubbed once and for all. Men are often too shy and opportunities are often missed because of that. Why should it be only men that have to leave themselves open to rejection? Remember men are vulnerable too.

12. ***The man should always pay for the meal.*** Oh Boy! We live in the days of equal opportunities and women earn good money, so why not let women pay for themselves? Most women can easily pay for themselves and would prefer to anyway, as it is less compromising.

13. ***It is selfish to put your own needs before others.*** This is a common one and not necessarily right. If you don't look after yourself, you may not be well enough or have enough energy to look after others. Remember that announcement they make on the aeroplane, 'In the unlikely event of an emergency, when the oxygen mask drops down, put your own on first and then you can help others'. And no one ever said 'Love thy neighbour better than thyself ', did they? 'As thyself' implies, or even assumes, that we are already loving ourselves.

14. ***To be a really worthwhile and worthy person, you must be up early in the morning.*** How often those friends of ours, who get up at the crack of dawn, will say with an air of superiority

'I get up at five thirty every morning'. They look askance at those of us who rise at eight-thirty, or even nine o'clock and there is a very subtle, and sometimes not-so-subtle, attempt to make us feel guilty. Ok, if you actually have to get up early or you even like getting up early, then it is understandable but there are those who don't have to do so and whose body-clock may be very differently regulated. I know of many creative and inventive people who get their best ideas late at night. So many writers admit to working well into the wee small hours, which may be where the expression 'burning the midnight oil' originates from. If they are writing, or painting or working on their inventions till three o'clock in the morning, how on earth can they be up at five thirty? The old saw, 'early to bed and early to rise, makes a man healthy, wealthy and wise', may have been entirely appropriate in rural farming communities of old, but does not apply across the board. Human biorhythms have identified the 'owls and larks' syndrome. Owls work best late in the day and larks are best in the morning. So, don't let the larks make the owls feel guilty!

> This, above all, to thine own self be true, thou canst not then be false to any man.
> William Shakespeare

15. ***Women over forty shouldn't have long hair.***
    Another all-sweeping generalisation! If you are over forty, fifty or sixty and your hair suits you

long, enjoy it. Look around you at the many examples of stunning older women with long hair. It suits them beautifully.

16. One of my clients, a very heterosexual man with a wife and four kids, in all seriousness, sent me his 'Silly Rule'. It was **'Men shouldn't wear skirts'.** I'm not sure what I think about that one. But who am I to judge? After all, I'm the proponent of the 'F**k It!' philosophy. And maybe he could wear a skirt if he wants to! He said he would really like it if men could do that. And they do in some cultures.

And on and on we go...

Most of the above were given to me by friends when I asked them for examples of what they thought were 'silly' rules. I'm sure you can think of a lot of your own.

Then, of course, there are lots of silly 'rules' that really come under the heading of superstitions, like, you shouldn't walk under a ladder. I have defied this silly 'rule' for decades and nothing untoward has ever happened to me because of it. The same applies to seeing one magpie on the road. To believe in these ridiculous superstitions is to really give our power away. Some would call it 'worshipping false gods'! Many years ago, my mother wore green to a cousin's wedding and was asked to leave because my cousin had the superstition that green was unlucky! Some people don't buy green cars. How in Heaven's name could green be unlucky? All around us nature, in all her glory, is mostly green and nature makes few mistakes. If you believe that green is unlucky (or red, or yellow or purple or any other colour) then that belief will attract misfortune. It is not the colour that does it; it's the belief. By our beliefs we create our reality.

Remember it's the belief that counts: Whatever we believe in we give power to.

In a Nutshell
Think for yourself. Examine the silly rules of 'the herd'. Don't be a sheep. Do only what feels right. Even if everyone else is doing it and you don't feel it's right for you; with good intentions to all, just adopt the 'F**k It!' attitude.

That's Freedom!
That's Power!
That's Greatness!

CHAPTER FIVE

Keeping it Simple

The 'F**k It!' way is all about simplicity. It's about dumping all sorts of 'shoulds', negative conditioning and unrealistic expectations. In fact, the whole of the 'F**k It!' way to success and happiness can be summed up in a few words; otherwise, we are missing the whole point.

So, very simply put, the 'F**k It!' way is to GET OUT OF OPERATING FROM EGO AND STEP INTO FUNCTIONING FROM HIGHER SELF.

That - just that - is the core of the whole thing. All the rest of this book is just window-dressing! Maybe some of the window-dressing is necessary information to help to explain the concept of ego and Higher Self. Maybe some is interesting and some may even be humorous and give you a laugh.

But, I repeat: the nub of the idea in this book is to… 'F**k It!'
Or 'Let god and let God'.
Or 'Get out of the driving seat'.
Or 'Hand your life over to a Higher Power'.

All one and the same thing; all the same concept.

Our programming for centuries has gone contrary to the idea of simplicity. The egos of so many people, down through the ages, have created a world of complexity and struggle. The idea has been fostered that for something to be worthwhile it should (that word again!) involve pain, hardship, hard work and struggle.

Pain and even poverty have been glorified but then that is all part of the insanity of the egoic mind. The egoic mind is the same insane mind that glorifies war and the 'glorious dead'! (What could be glorious about being dead?) The ego really is insane.

If you sent off for a course on how to improve your life, you paid a lot of money for this course and it entailed countless hours of study and hard work and never-ending modules to get through, the egoic mind would consider this worthwhile and a worthy way forward. But to suggest that all you have to do is 'Let go and let Source' or 'F**k It!' Now that's going against all the ego's principles. Of course it is, as the ego will lose power that way and the ego can't have that!

Malcolm!
Remember what the psychologist Jung said, 'What you resist, persists', so when we resist the ego, it will kick up a hell of a stink. The best strategy with the ego is to include it, to appease it. Getting the ego and the Higher Self to work together is the best bet. It is also the way

to heal the division in who we are: to become whole, instead of being fractured
and splintered.

      I am quite a visual person and I think a lot in pictures. For some bizarre reason I see my ego as a little snotty urchin; he looks like a character from Oliver Twist and I call him Malcolm! Crazy? Do whatever it takes, whatever works for you. I try to 'mother' Malcolm and I have little inner mental chats with him and I say things like 'O.K Malcolm.
Thank you for sharing your fears with me, but WE are going to be all right.' (I wonder if that is how the royal 'we' came about. Did they know something we don't know?)

      In this way, Malcolm becomes appeased and becomes an ally rather than a saboteur. The Hawaiian Kahunas had a similar concept for this 'little self'. Their knowledge of the layers within the persona was the basis for their hugely effective methods of healing and manifestation. The ego is
like a child; self-centred, fearful, prideful and lacking in wisdom, and yet that is the part of us, which is usually in charge. It is in charge without our knowing it, as we sleepwalk through life. No wonder that most people's lives are in chaos. Once we do wake up from that sleepwalking state we are in, life takes on new meaning and we cannot operate in the old way ever again. To stay awake Is essential and for that we need to shake ourselves out of old habits and from mind numbing exercises like watching junk on TV. Most of the

repetitious rubbish on TV is 'chewing gum for the mind' and serves no useful purpose at all.

Nowadays, since my defining 'F**k It!' moment, I continuously ask myself 'who is in the driving seat?' It is important to be awake and aware but not to struggle. When the fear of lack of money rears its ugly head, I know that is ego. The Higher Self knows nothing of lack and therefore cannot create it. The switch has to be made then from operating from the limited little ego and letting the unlimited Higher Self take over; without stress or strain. The same principle works for illness or any other problem. It is not always easy to go against a lifetime of conditioning, but as I do a mental shrug and say 'F**k It!' to the problem and hand it over. The Higher Self finds a way to rectify it and I don't have to put in effort. All I have to do is get out of my own ego way. Easy Peasy!

'F**K It!' in the Workplace

Now, some may think this implies that you just say 'F**k It!' hand in your notice at work and let the universe provide. It is not quite like that. I am a great believer in 'God helps those who help themselves'. If you hate your job, hand the situation over to your Higher Self; stay in the job, do the very best you can while you are there and, before you know it, if you have let your Higher Self take charge, a new opportunity or a new job will present itself and, as your Higher Self put it your way, you can bet it will be a good one.

In the matter of relationships at work, if there is rancour, recognise that it is because there are egos involved. Withdraw from the competition or the need to be right (ego stuff) and bring in the quiet wisdom and compassion of the Higher Self. You may find that, as you change, the situation changes. It's bound to! This does not mean you have to be a doormat, but be bigger than the problem, rise above the pettiness; don't give the pettiness energy.

If you are feeling hurt, look at why. It is not that we ought to deny how we feel. Feel the feelings but work out where they are coming from. Only the ego can feel hurt or put down or unappreciated, so bring your awareness to the highest within you and wait for the change to happen. 'F**k It!' and see! Always, always, when we hand over to the Higher Self, things work out beautifully.

'Fk It!' in Personal Relationships**
The ego has a field day when it comes to personal relationships. Here is where it goes to town on asserting itself and, in so doing, getting into some major insanity. The ego has a need to be right; a need to be loved; a need to be approved of and a mega need for attention. The word 'need' is the giveaway. The Higher Self has no need of anything, it HAS everything; it is self-contained. Two people, operating from ego in a relationship, are not likely to have a marriage made in Heaven. And, by the way, Heaven is not a place; it is a state of consciousness. When one or both of the partners can operate from the level of Higher Self then there is a greater chance of happiness. A friend of mine used to have a plaque on her wall which said 'Two half people don't make a whole, but two whole people make a

beautiful relationship', which just about sums up the situation. To be truly whole we have to operate from our Higher Selves and not from ego.

It is sad that so many of our country and western songs and our pop songs emphasise the 'need' factor in love. 'I need you.' 'Feel the need in me.' And a lot of our previous conceptions of love were based on the premise of half a person, i.e. 'the other half', or 'my better half'. 'I'll be complete when I meet my other half.' Sad! Sad! Sad!

If both partners are operating from Higher Self, most of the time or for a major part of the time, there is every chance of a lasting and happy relationship. When there is a crisis in a relationship (and there are bound to be crises from time to time, as most of us are still a long way off from operating from Higher Self all the time), we slip in and out of ego again and again. Then, if we can focus on Higher Self and ask it to take over, the Higher Self will bring wisdom and will try to understand the other person. The ego will go into blame and 'being right'. Ask yourself is it better to be right or to be happy? Always examine where you are coming from (ego or Higher Self), then when a relationship hits a troubled spot, if you can both make the gear shift from ego to Higher Self, harmony will soon be restored.

Two half people don't make a whole, but two whole people make a beautiful relationship.
Anon

'F**k It!' in Money Matters

Remember, the ego thinks in limitation and lack, so if you are experiencing limitation or lack right now, you're sure to know who is in charge! Change it! Shift gear! Give the management of your financial affairs over to the abundant and unlimited Higher Self. Adopt the 'F**k It!' attitude to the ego's little game. Call the ego's bluff. Hand over to Higher Self, relax and follow the intuitive guidance your amazing Higher Self will send you. Be prepared for unexpected opportunities appearing as if from nowhere and never, ever doubt. If doubt creeps in, it is a sign that the ego is creeping in by the back door and trying to take over again. Have a loving chat with your own personal 'Malcolm'. Relax! Let go! 'F**k It!'

The egoic mind really tries to get in control where questions of money are concerned. Remember, it operates from a viewpoint of lack and limitation. It will make us feel worried, frightened and concerned when money is scarce and will try to make us feel guilty when we have money. There is nothing virtuous about being poor, being poor is actually a 'sin', as we have missed the point; we have forgotten our true essence. Neither should we feel guilty when we have money, Stuart Wilde says 'The best thing you can do for the poor, is not to be one of them.' This is true as; if we are poor, we can't help anyone. Think of all the good you could do if you had money. Not having money and spending all our time worrying about it, stops us from being all that we are capable of being: all our Creator intended us to be. Money is energy; it is empowering. The Higher Self knows no lack.

The best thing you can do for the poor is not to be one of them.
Stuart Wilde.

'F**k It!' in Health

Again, it's the ego that brings on 'dis-ease' by negative doubts and fears. It is scientifically proven now that most disease is brought about more by attitude and thinking than by germs. Thousands of hours have been spent on research into this angle of how our thoughts and moods affect our health. There are countless books on the subject. All we have to do again is to bring in the Higher Self and operate from there and from there only. Think only health and, for goodness sake, stop worrying about your illness. Remember the affirmation 'I love being healthy' or 'Being healthy is great'. Making the affirmation keeps the ego mind busy while the Higher Self is getting on with the job of restoring us to our true state, which is one of health and vitality.

Years of old, unconscious programming may mean that you already have ailments which are well set into your body, even those will respond to the Higher Self's attention. You may have been born with ailments, so maybe you cannot be completely cured but you can be healed; your attitude to your ailment can be healed. You may acquire a new degree of acceptance and peace with your malady.

Acceptance can be a form of healing. A truly conscious connection to, coupled with unshakable faith in, the Higher Self can cause miracles to occur too; there are many well documented cases of this happening. How many of us are really capable of that degree of connection and faith? It is not out of our reach if only we relax, let go, put our health problem entirely in the hands of that which knows only health, i.e. Source, then we can be open to miracles happening. They do, all the time.

The ego is very sneaky, remember it wants to be in charge at any price, so it may tell you that you brought your illness on yourself by your wrong thinking and it will try to make you feel guilty. Guilt is not of the Higher Self, so if you are feeling it, let it go and hand everything - absolutely everything - over to your wonderful, all-powerful Higher Self.
And as for the limitations and limited thinking... 'F**k It!'

The 'F**k It!' Diet

There is no love sincerer than the love of food.
George Bernard Shaw

You've probably heard of the F-Plan diet, now here is the 'F**k It!' Plan!

Weight loss and diet are an endemic obsession in our society today. Diets and slimming clubs are big business. Every year someone comes up with a 'new and revolutionary' diet; this is the one that will change your life, they claim. We rush out to buy the book or the product or both and spend endless time in supermarkets looking at labels and examining the ingredients in everything we buy. The issue is on our minds day and night. We weigh, we measure, and we starve ourselves of what we really like. We feel deprived. We spend a huge amount of our time in a state of angst and worry. The whole thing becomes an obsessive addictive process.

For me, therapy junkie that I used to be, diets were another of my ways of struggling to improve my image. For more than thirty years, I tried a succession of different diets and regimes. They all worked... for a while! And, then – as I have the will power of a small flea - I would be tempted by some goodie and fall off the regime. The pounds would all come back on again, I'd feel a failure again, the guilt trip would set in and I would feel worse than before. What an endless treadmill of frustration! I sometimes felt there was no way out.

Believe it or not, the 'F**K It!' moment I had last year, not only brought about huge positive changes in my life, generally, but it brought a flash of insight to the diet issue as well. This new understanding for me, of ego and Higher Self, worked right across the board. The ego believes in struggle and limitation and was getting a great power trip out of the endless diets. Every new diet would bring hope, the failure followed and then guilt set in and the ego was having a ball.

All these diets worked for a while. Of course, they did because they were based on belief. We are sold an idea that this new revolutionary diet is the diet to end all diets. We believe it, because we want to. The sales talk is so good that we are convinced. Even some of the proponents of the various diets are convinced themselves. Hyped-up on the belief that the diet works, it actually does, for a while, as long as the belief is still strong. All the diets work, despite the fact that they are based on different and often contradictory concepts. There's the Atkins high protein diet, which is all protein and hardly any carbohydrate, then there's the Pasta diet; all carbohydrate and hardly any protein. There's the F-Plan diet, with lots of bulk, and all the low calorie diets, which have hardly any bulk at all. No wonder we get confused! Every dieter you talk to has his or her own conviction.

All the diets work for a while but are bound to fail in the end because the egoic mind is obsessed with WEIGHT; WEIGHT loss! WEIGHT watching! losing WEIGHT! We know that what we focus on, we get more of. The thoughts we entertain are far more important than anything we take through our mouths. Why didn't I recognise that simple fact before now? The only way to crack the issue is to focus on being SLIM. Think SLIM! Talk SLIM!

Everything in the universe is energy and that includes food. Food, at its basic atomic level, is energy. That energy is amenable to our thoughts. We are the creators of our own reality.

Now I have turned the whole issue of my body image over to my Higher Self. My Higher Self prompts me to focus on SLIMNESS and, to my delight; my body is slowly getting closer to the shape and size I desire. Not only that, but I eat what I like. Music to the ears of this chocoholic!

There is so much out there to see and feel and taste; all part of the banquet our Creator gave us. What a pity to live in deprivation and denial. Better to appreciate the infinite variety of wonderful things that are on offer on this wonderful planet; to enjoy the feast created for us.

So, as far as diets are concerned 'F**k It!' Enjoy your food, feed and nurture all your friends with delicious taste bud sensations. There is something so loving, warm and nurturing about preparing delightful food and sharing it with those we love.

So enjoy! Think SLIM and be happy!

If more of us valued food and cheer and song above hoarded gold, it would be a merrier world.
J.R.R. Tolkien

In a Nutshell
Whatever area of your life is giving you problems there is one sure answer: Stop operating from ego and shift gear to working from Higher Self. Hand your life and all its concerns over to Higher Self. Higher Self is a fragment of Source. 'Made in the image and likeness of Source.'

Higher Self is unlimited.

Anne Hassett

CHAPTER SIX

Laughter and Fun

I think it was Oscar Wilde who said 'Life is too serious to be taken seriously'.

And how true that is! Walk along any street and look at people's expressions; how few look happy. Observe people in their cars, in traffic queues; the anxiety and seriousness in their faces is a sad reflection of the human condition.

Is life really to be taken so seriously? Absolutely not! As beings of limitlessness and light, we originally came into the physical universe to explore and to have fun. We came on a great adventure. But, Boy, haven't we got ourselves caught up in the play: in the illusion! By remembering the truth of who we are, and by operating from our Higher Selves, we could change it all so easily. All we have to do is wake up, remember who we are and live lightly and with joy.

There will be a lot of people out there, who are operating from their fearful egoic minds, who will tell you that you can't do that. They will tell you that you must be deadly serious about everything and that life is a serious business. Of course, they are right. If you think and believe that life is a serious business, then it is. On the contrary, if you think life is fun, then it is. Remember what Henry Ford said, 'Whether you think you can or you think you can't, either way you are right'. Henry knew the secret of the mind; that what we think, we create. And we do have choices; we have the choice to change our beliefs and perceptions. Life boils down to what's in the mind; to what our beliefs are. Change attitude and life changes.

Not a shred of evidence exists in favour of the idea that life is serious.
Brendan Gill.

We CAN have fun doing our job. Someone once said to me 'the secret to success in life is to do what makes your heart sing'. That was one of the best bits of advice I have ever had. Thankfully, I now do what makes my heart sing and I love my life. I do what I love; I get paid for doing it and get to travel all over the world and to meet lovely people. That was not always so. Way back - many years ago - I took a leap of faith and life has gone from good to better to absolutely great! And even better still since my 'F**k it!' moment!

I meet so many people who are in jobs they hate, so they clock-watch all day; they count the hours until Friday and loathe Monday mornings. This is hardly a happy or healthy way to live life. When asked why they don't make a change, they have scores of excuses. 'My husband wouldn't like it.' 'I have paid a lot into my pension.' 'I'm too old to get another job.' 'I wouldn't be able to make a living at what I really want to do.'

Excuses! Excuses! Excuses! In those situations, if we decide what we really want to do, turn the situation over to the Higher Self, get the ego out of the way and then wait for the opening, it will surely come. The Higher Self will find a way. The Higher Self delights in seeing us become who we truly are. It is often the dreams we had in childhood which hold the clue as to our true purpose in life. Sadly, we get side-tracked as we grow older and lose sight of ourselves. Remember, it is never too late to do or to be what you want to be. There are inspiring examples all around us, like Mary Wesley, who didn't start writing until she was seventy and wrote several bestselling novels, some of which were turned into TV films. And Grandma Moses, who didn't start painting until she was eighty-two. Ageism is another of the ego's limiting ploys.

Those who love what they do, don't see it as work; they are immersed in the enjoyment of whatever it is they are doing and, consequently, time flies. These people even look forward to what new experiences Monday morning may bring. They love what they are doing so much that they don't mind putting in the extra hours so, inevitably, they make more money. They want to be the best; they want to produce the best; they take a pride in themselves and what they do. They are expressing their Divine Essence. These are people who are truly connected to their inner creative spirit; their Higher Self.

That's the 'F**k It!' way!

Laughter

We have all heard the old saying 'Laughter is the best medicine'. When did you last have a really good belly laugh? When was the last time you had tears running down your face at something that made you laugh so much? Remember how good it felt. That feeling filled you with exuberance and lifted your spirits. We now know that laughter produces a chemical reaction, which affects our mood and creates well-being. Laughter is contagious. Notice that when someone is laughing uncontrollably, even if you don't know what they are laughing at, you can't help but join in. Laughter lightens up the world and helps to make life more positive. Laughter releases tension in our bodies and in tense situations.

In the best seller DVD, *The Secret*, there is a story of a lady who claims to have cured herself of cancer by watching funny movies all day, every day, until she was well. She literally laughed herself to health. Norman Cousins recovered from a crippling disease in much the same way. In his book, *Anatomy of an illness*, he says his main medicine was large doses of laughs. He watched Marx Brothers and *Candid Camera* tapes until he got better. Laughter relieves pain; endorphins are released in the brain when we laugh and this creates a natural high. Conversely, we can make ourselves ill by taking life too seriously and being miserable. So, 'F**k It!' Have a good laugh instead.

Ease

Easy does it! Learning to pace ourselves and get in the flow of life produces amazing results. As we do that, we make the connection to Source/All-That-Is/the Field-of-all-possibilities. The flow of the universe has a rhythm to it. Pacing ourselves is going with the flow.

Don't push the river.
Shirley MacLaine

Trees don't try to grow, they just do it. The earth spins without effort. Birds fly, fish swim, hearts beat, lungs breathe, our hair and nails grow and all in perfect harmony and effortlessness. Isn't it great that there is a Power, which oversees all this? If our collective egos were in charge, we'd be in a right old mess!

Effortlessness is nature's way. In the ancient Vedic writings of India, they referred to this principle of effortlessness as that of 'doing less and accomplishing more'. The Viking runic wisdom says 'Do without doing and everything gets done'. Jesus said 'of myself I can do nothing, it is the father in me that doeth the works'. He was referring to the Higher Self, that part of each of us, which is a part of Source. Father was a word that people of that time could understand. Our Higher Self is like a loving parent to us: a wise and caring parent. It is, after all, part of the Source from which we spring, and we are the offspring or children of Source. When we hand over to our Higher Self and get in sync, we flourish.

Live life with passion and never with haste.
Anne Hassett

Fun

Fun is such a tonic. Children know how to have fun. We, as adults, have become so self-conscious that we have a problem letting our hair down. Our little ego selves are so caught up in 'not making fools of ourselves' that, instead, we are all uptight and rigid. We say we are shy. It took me a long time to realise that shyness is really a form of arrogance; the idea that everyone was looking at ME! Why did I think I was so important?

Let your hair down. 'F**k It!' Dance! Jump in puddles! Buy yourself a balloon! Smile at strangers! Sing in the lift! Hum on the train! Wear bright colours! Throw a fancy dress party! Build a sandcastle on the beach! (Don't just wait until you have the children with you as an excuse, pretending the sandcastle is for them!) Be a child again! If people laugh at us while we act the fool, won't it give them something to smile about? We could do a lot worse! We might just brighten up their day. The Higher Self loves to express joy, whatever it takes.

The ego hates to be an object of ridicule. When I am feeling self-conscious, I know I am operating from ego. When operating from Higher Self the opinions of others are immaterial. Real freedom is not having to be validated by anyone else's opinion. It is real liberty when we approve of ourselves and don't have to wait for the approval of others. As long as we are not harming another, anything goes.

Getting embarrassed is another sign of the ego's paranoia. We can loosen the ego's stranglehold when we can laugh at our own embarrassing situations.

Boys, if you notice your flies are undone, when you are standing up to make an important speech in public, just turn around and adjust them, then turn back, make a joke of it and carry on regardless. And girls, if you emerge from the loo, walk half way down the restaurant and realise your skirt is all caught up in your knickers, pull it down, smile and take a bow.
Then walk on. Everyone makes mistakes, not getting all hot and bothered about them takes the sting out of them and everyone will forget almost immediately. We really are not that important to other people!

Make sure that there are times for fun scheduled into your life; the more fun you have, the more time you'll want to make for it. Get out there and live life with enthusiasm!

Life is a great big canvas; throw all the paint you can at it.
Danny Kaye

Gratitude
I used to know an amazing Australian lady, who has now passed on. She used to say 'You can't be depressed and grateful at the same time'. So, if you're feeling depressed, and everyone feels depressed now and again, mentally start being grateful. You'll find that very soon your spirits will lift, as you begin to realise how lucky you are and the depression will have diminished or disappeared entirely.

The really pessimistic will say 'But I have nothing to be grateful for'. Maybe one could just be grateful for being alive, having eyes to see with, being able to walk, being able to talk, having food and shelter, living in a country that is not at war... and the list goes on. When we wake up in the morning, we can be grateful for having had a good night's sleep, or if we haven't, we can at least be grateful for having a bed to sleep in. Many haven't. And, if you haven't got a bed to sleep in, how did you afford to buy this book? At night, we can focus on the good things that have happened during the day and say 'Thanks' for them. There is always something to be grateful for and as one focuses on what is good in life, it is impossible to be depressed. And there is the added bonus that what one focuses on, one gets more of. Body language too is helpful when depression comes along; it is very difficult to be depressed with one's chin up and head held high, just as it is nearly impossible to be happy or optimistic when we adopt the posture of slumped shoulders and head hanging down. Try it and see!

Gratitude is not only the greatest of virtues, but the parent of all others.
Cicero

Have a 'gratitude binge'. Start by being grateful for all the good in your life. Give thanks for your family and friends, how well your body works, the wonderful holidays you have had, the home you live in; add your own things to the list. You'll be surprised. Not only that, but you'll feel tons better afterwards and, of course, what you focus on, you get more of. The latter is the most fundamental law of the universe: the Law of Attraction.

An attitude of gratitude will put a sparkle in your eyes and a spring in your step. Other people will notice and they will be attracted to you because you are radiating a very special positive energy.

As your gratitude expands, you will literally become 'high' on life. You will feel an invigorating energy charge through your body. Your health will improve and you will become a magnet for the right people and the right opportunities in life.

'F**k It!' Life is too short to be dour, miserable and sad.

In a Nutshell
When you are on course in life, your heart will sing. It is never too late to live your dream. Laugh. Enjoy. And trust the Source of all good. Adopt an attitude of gratitude.

Anne Hassett

CHAPTER SEVEN

The Mofia

No, it is not a misspelling; you got it right first time, it's the Mofia. Who are they? They are the 'Masters Of 'F**k It!' Attitude'. M.O.F.I.A.

You will see these people around you here and there. They are easy to recognise. They are more than likely to be successful at what they do.
They do jobs that make their hearts sing.
They really enjoy what they do, so they are at the top of their particular tree.
They move about with a bounce in their step and a smile on their face.
They have charisma. Charisma was originally a spiritual term, which meant 'of the spirit'. Because they have charisma, Mofias are attractive to people and are popular wherever they go. They are always in great demand.
They don't take themselves too seriously.
They don't mind making fools of themselves. When they do something that others consider ridiculous, the Mofia will just shrug his or her shoulders and get on with life.
They 'live and let live'.
They don't judge or condemn others.

They don't deliberately hurt others but they don't compromise themselves to suit others either.
Mofias are true to themselves and to their own ideals.
They have enthusiasm for life.
They have 'gusto'.
They are in the flow and achieve with ease and without stress.
They surf the waves of the energy of life.
They get in the flow and they go with the flow. Of course, they recognise where the flow is because they are 'connected'. (Connected to their Higher Selves.)
When things don't go according to plan for Mofias, they just shrug their shoulders and say 'F**k It!' knowing that, as they are connected to their Higher Selves, new and even better opportunities will come along presently.
Mofias know their true essence as Unlimited Beings connected to (and part of) the Field of Infinite Possibilities.
When ego-driven, fearful folk say to a Mofia 'Get real' or 'Be realistic', as these fearful folk are wont to do, the Mofia will not enter into argument or explanation, as the Mofia knows that what is really 'real' is the miraculous. What is 'real' to the ego is the appearance before it and not the true reality behind it.
Mofias love beauty. They surround themselves with it; they see beauty in all, even the most mundane of things.
Mofias help others, quietly, often without getting found out. They don't do it for glory, praise, or ego.
Mofias avoid low energy people, places and situations.
They know that everything in the universe is energy and that this energy vibrates at different levels. They know

that to better attract high energy situations in life they must avoid low energy.

Mofias attract high energy with laughter, love and fun. They are entirely optimistic. Their ego-driven colleagues and friends may accuse them of having a 'Pollyanna' attitude to life, but the Mofias understand the Law of Attraction and they know that it works every time, so they look for the best and expect the best and, consequently, they get the best.

> *The glory of God is a human who is fully alive.*
> Irish Saint

Mofias don't worship false gods. They know that all power comes from Source through their Higher Selves, so they don't give their power away to foods that may be 'bad' for them or to 'Draughts that may give them a cold' or to the belief that flu is inevitable 'because there's a bug going around'. They know that, through the Law of Attraction, to
think negative thoughts will bring about negative results.

Mofias know that when doubts such as these creep in, it is the ego at work. They quickly catch this way of thinking; they change gear and switch to operating from the limitless Higher Self. Mofias trust their Higher Selves to take care of them.

Mofias know that, as we are made in the image and likeness of Source, we have access to all that Source is.

We are in life to learn. We are here to move from victimhood to mastery. The Mofias are the ones who've cracked it. Mofias are an expression of the Glory of God.

'F**k It!' Join the Mofia.

In a Nutshell
Join the ranks of those who have made it. Join the Mofia. They are the Masters Of 'F**k It!' Attitude.

M.O.F.I.A.

MOFIAS RULE O.K !

CHAPTER EIGHT

Paradigm Shift

The 'F**K It!' way to success and happiness is a simple and very easy one but it involves a major shift in behaviour and attitude. Letting go of the ego's way of working and handing over to a power that is greater than our little selves, is such an unfamiliar concept to most people. For many people, they may not even want to take that leap into the unknown until the going gets really tough. But isn't that a pity! Why wait until everything is falling down around your ears to 'let go and let God?' The ego has had such a hold on us for so long that it seems normal to operate from there. All we have to do is look around us and see the state of the world to realise that operating from ego isn't actually working. It may seem to work sometimes but so many people are unhappy and their lives are lived in a state of constant anxiety.

It could all be so different!

Soul Search!
Have a stock-take of your life. Is it really working the way you want it to? Are you happy? Are you fulfilled? Are you living to work or working to live? Is life one long treadmill of struggle and anxiety? Are you at peace in

your inner being? How often can you sit still and just be? Are you constantly on the run? Do you think you might just be running away from yourself?

Are you someone who can't bear to be alone? If you are, ask yourself what are you frightened of? Do you have to fill every waking hour with activity? If the answer is 'yes' to that, maybe you are running away from your pain, afraid to face your own inner thoughts. Do you sometimes feel that there will never be enough or that what you have may not last long enough? (Love, money, health, good looks, youth, friends, energy.)

Is there something you have always wanted to do but were afraid to do it because... We all find our own 'becauses'! Then there's a very good chance that your ego has a stranglehold on your life. It is surely time to have a jolly good palaver with your ego (your own personal Malcolm!) and get a few things straightened out. It is time
to relinquish ego control and align with Source by handing everything over to the Higher Self. The handing over needs to be complete, no holds barred. Then Higher Self will sort out all the inner pain, the shame we have held on to (consciously or unconsciously) for years; the fears we have about not having enough money or about growing old or not being loved, or whatever our particular weak spot is. The Higher Self will make all things new; and will do it easily and effortlessly. The only effort we have to put into it is to watch out for the clever and conniving ego's attempts to slip back in by the back door. So, just for the effort of a little vigilance, there is huge reward.

Time for YOUR 'F**K It!' moment! Go on! try it! You won't be sorry, as your life will take on a new and unbelievably different and better dimension.

Love

Live, love, laugh and be happy.
From a nineteen-forties song

What is love? If you can answer that one then you are answering the sixty-four thousand dollar question! So many things are labelled as 'love' that have very little relation to it at all. Gratuitous sex, for example, is often referred to as 'making love', when there is so often very little love involved in it. Why not call a spade a spade and call it having sex? Sex without love involved is pure physical gratification and neither bad nor good, just the feeding of an appetite. Why do we need to dress it up? Sex, when love is involved, can be akin to a spiritual experience and can take the participants to great heights of ecstasy; and once experienced, never forgotten.

There is mother love and love of family members for one another; love of friends for friends; love for animals and pets. There is love for country and love for groups and causes; love for God or for the angels. Indeed there are many kinds of love.

There is also love for self. This love for self is not the egoic love of oneself, which can be selfish and arrogant. The real love for self is that compassion for oneself, where one can accept oneself, warts and all. Without the latter, it is difficult (if not impossible) to truly love others.

All you need is love.
The Beatles

Unconditional love is the only REAL love. Love which has conditions attached is not love at all but some feeling posing as love. When we have strings attached to our 'love' for someone it is not love at all but something else. How often do we say 'I will love him if he behaves himself', or 'I love her when she is being reasonable'. Real love is compassionate acceptance of the other person without agenda or expectation or judgement. Tall order, Huh?

'F**k It!' Try a little unconditional love and see what happens. You may be agreeably surprised. And don't forget to include yourself in this; your real self is perfect and, therefore, very worthy of love; it IS love. The ego is like a child (immature spiritually) and can be loved like a child.
Show patience and compassion for your ego by the wisest, most loving aspect of yourself. By showing love for the erring and limited ego aspect, a loving union can take place, which heals the dichotomy in ourselves. Fill your life with love in every way you can.

Prayer
What is prayer?
Prayer is a form of intention. Thought itself is prayer.

What thoughts we send out impress upon the substance or 'Godness', which is everywhere around us and returns what we send out. If we worry it is a form of prayer, but because of its negative nature, it is not to be recommended!

Conscious prayer is making the connection to Higher Self and then, through Higher Self, to Source/All-That-Is. Prayer does not need to be formal or to be ritualised. We can talk to our Higher Self as we would to a friend and our Higher Self is the best friend we can have because it IS us; it is that part of us outside of time and space, connected to Source.

We are usually so disconnected from our Higher Self that we cannot avail of all that is our birthright but, as we make the conscious connection, the blessings begin to flow in. We can make that conscious connection either through prayer or through meditation. When we are struggling to make that connection, if our desire to do so is sincere, our Higher Self will come half way to meet us. This is where the Father comes half way to meet the Prodigal Son and as they are reunited, the Father showers the Prodigal Son with untold gifts and blessings. So it is for us when we have an earnest desire to heal the separation in ourselves and, consequently, between ourselves and Source; not only are all things made new but they overflow in untold blessings and wondrous ways.

What we have previously thought of as prayer, the mindless repetition of words we learned long ago, is of very little use. How could it be? The mind and the heart are not involved, nor are we even conscious of what we are saying. Rather than the insincere parrot fashion repeating of formula-type recitations, we would gain much more from a heartfelt 'Please help me God'. No sincere prayer ever goes unanswered. Words and thoughts that are sent from our hearts to a Higher Power do not return void.

There have been scientific studies done on the power of prayer. Sick people, who were prayed for, recovered more quickly than the control group who were not.

Pray for yourself. Take your thoughts and desires and place them on the altar of your innermost being. It is the Father's good pleasure to give you the kingdom. Pray for others in the same way. When praying for others, we need to be careful about being specific, as what we wish for them may not be for their highest good. Even in a situation where someone is dying of an illness, it may not be for their highest good that they remain on earth. We cannot judge what is best for another soul. The best prayer for them is to say something like 'Love and Light to (name) and may he/she be at peace'. We can use the same prayer, if we wish, to send healing to a troubled situation, either in our own lives or in the world at large.

As we are all connected, albeit unconsciously, what we do for others we do for ourselves. My wish of peace for others can only bring peace to me too.

The kneeling-down, pleading to an outside God for help is not the way of true prayer, as that only perpetuates the sense of separation (or sin) from Source/God. Source/ God is within us and all around us: the Holy Spirit within. The ego thinks it is separate, which of course it is not, but it thinks so and therefore fosters a sense of duality and separation. True prayer is to connect to Spirit. To truly connect is the greatest prayer and the conduit for miracles.

When praying, don't try too hard. Have the intention to return or to connect with Higher Self and then, as in the story of the Prodigal Son, the Father/Source will come out to meet you half way. It is really very easy and very simple, as all true things are.

In a Nutshell
Making a conscious connection with the Source of our being is the best form of prayer.
When connected, ask and it is given.
No true prayer ever goes unanswered.

Anne Hassett

CHAPTER NINE

Kernels

We've had a lot of 'nutshells' along the way. So what about them? What's in them? Funny we should be on a 'nut' theme, as we are all nuts when we operate from ego. The ego is basically insane. It sees not reason. It's views and opinions and attitude to life are all askew. Let's have a look at these 'nutshells' again and prise the kernels out of them...

Nutshell
Recognise the expressions and levels of your being: ego and Higher Self. The ego is limited and when we operate from ego, we can only be limited. The Higher Self is unlimited and operating from the Higher Self creates unlimited wellbeing, joy, abundance and love.
Kernel
In other words... know who and what you truly are.

Nutshell
When we come to accept that there is an All-Intelligent and Unlimited Power in the Universe, that we are part of and can connect to, we can 'plug in' and download from this unlimited reservoir of all good things. Then life becomes unimaginably wonderful. It is really, very simple.

Kernel
Know that there is an Unlimited Power and connect with it.

Nutshell
Don't entertain problems; they make rotten house-guests. Focus on what you want and not on what you don't want. Let go of overwork. Live in the now and trust the Higher Self to provide. Enjoy life. Be a human 'being' and not a human 'doing'.

Kernel
Focus only on the positive. Trust Higher Self. Relax and enjoy life.

Nutshell
Think for yourself. Examine the silly rules of 'the herd'. Don't be a sheep. Do only what feels right. Even if everyone else is doing it and you don't feel it's right for you; with good intentions to all, just adopt the 'F**k It!' attitude.

> That's Freedom!
> That's Power!
> That's Greatness!

Kernel.
Be true to yourself. Don't be one of the 'herd'.

Nutshell
Whatever area of your life is giving you problems there is one sure answer; Stop operating from ego and shift gear to working from Higher Self. Hand your life and all its concerns over to Higher Self. Higher Self is a fragment of Source. 'Made in the image and likeness of Source.'

Higher Self is unlimited.
Kernel
Get out of the driving seat. Hand over. Let go and let
God/Higher Self.
*'F**k It!'*

Nutshell
When you are on course in life, your heart will sing. It is
never too late to live your dream. Laugh. Enjoy. And
trust the Source of all good. Adopt an attitude of
gratitude.
Kernel
Live, love, laugh and be happy. Be grateful.

Nutshell
Join the ranks of those who have made it. Join the
Mofia. They are the Masters Of 'F**k It!' Attitude.
M.O.F.I.A.
Kernel
*Basically - 'F**k It!'*

Nutshell
Making a conscious connection with the Source of our
being is the best form of prayer.
When connected, ask and it is given.
No true prayer ever goes unanswered.
Kernel
Plug in to Source and ask. Trust and it will come.

Kernel of this Entire Book
So, the kernel (dictionary meaning of 'kernel' is nucleus;
essence; core) of this book goes back to what I said in

Chapter Five: GET OUT OF OPERATING FROM EGO AND
STEP INTO FUNCTIONING FROM HIGHER SELF.
Or 'Let go and let God'.
Or hand your life over to a Higher Power.

And just - to the ego and the problems and all
the ego's games and power plays and fears and
shenanigans – say 'F**k It!'

And when the going gets tough and the ego
snidely sneaks back into the driving seat again, catch it
and let go again. Give up control! hand over! 'F**k it!'

The element of risk perceived in stepping from
ego living to Higher Self living is huge if you've never
tried it before. Go on, try it; what have you got to lose?

Let go. And keep letting go. Wait for the
miracles to happen, as they surely will.

A Suggested Prayer
The One Great Power of the Universe is in, around and
through me now. This Loving Power is individualised as
me. As I totally and unconditionally surrender
everything in my life to this Awesome Power, my body
receives healing, all my relationships are brought into
harmony, my financial affairs are prospered in truly
miraculous ways and all crooked parts of my life are
made straight. Through the power of intention, I
connect to this Mighty Power. I surrender my
personality, my mind and my ego. I now believe that
Source (you may use the word 'God' here if you wish) is
the only Power in all aspects of my life and therefore
only good can come to me. With all my heart, I give

thanks to this Loving Power for the miracles that now appear in my life.
Amen.

Anne Hassett

Postscript

One of my friends, who read the draft copy of this book, said 'Anne, aren't you going to mention what is happening in today's world; how we can save the planet?'

No. I am not. Why? Because we can only save ourselves - each one of us. It is through saving ourselves that we save the whole. We are all cells in one great Being. To put the saving of others first is taking responsibility for others' growth and evolution and is therefore co-dependency. By all and every means, help everyone you can but without imposing or interfering. A great teacher once said 'I am not my brother's keeper'. In the light of today's knowledge, we now have an understanding of that statement.

Someone, maybe it was Ghandi (I can seldom remember who said what, only what they said!), said 'Let there be peace, but let it begin with me'.

We must start right here, in our own consciousness and heal our separation from Source by remembering who we are. We must move to being our own Divine Self and diminish the power of the ego. Like Mother Teresa, we must see the Divine in all others too and, if given the opportunity, remind them of who they really are.

As each of us heals ourselves and operates from Higher Self rather than from ego, then and only then, can we heal the world. Embrace the ego too. It is part of you. Love your own personal 'Malcolm'. (By now I'm sure you have found your own name for your ego.) Embrace your ego but take charge; step into your power. Remember your 'godness'.

As we actually become, or should I say return to, our Higher Selves, then love, health and abundance of all kinds MUST be the nature of our reality. As the power of the ego, and all the other egos, falls away, so does fear, greed, war and want. The latter are all constructs of the ego. The Higher Self (and remember all our Higher Selves) is part of the One Self/Source and the One Higher Self knows only perfection. As this One Higher Power is unlimited, we can, as one, perform miracles.

I truly believe that now is the time of the great awakening. When you look around and see the appearance of chaos, you may be filled with dismay. But, think again; could it not be the last desperate stand of the ego, and all the egos who see the writing on the wall, as we start to remember who we really are? All the doubts and fears of the ages are coming to the surface to be cleared once and for all time.

This is a time of remembering our glorious origin. A time of healing the separation.

We stand on the threshold of a golden era.

NAMASTE!
(Namaste means 'I salute the Divine in you'.)

Suggested Reading

Empowerment
John Randolph Price (Quartus)

Illusions
Richard Bach (Pan Books)

Excuse Me, Your Life is Waiting
Lynn Grabhorn (Hampton Roads)

The Field
Lynne Mc Taggart (Element Books)

The Nature of Personal Reality
Jane Roberts (New World Library)

Find And Use Your Inner Power
Emmet Fox (Harper Collins)

The Isaiah Effect
Gregg Braden (Hay House)

The Power of Your Subconscious Mind
Dr. Joseph Murphy (Bantam Books)

The Only Diet There Is
Sondra Ray (Celestial Arts)

Other books by Anne Hassett:

'Reading Your Child's Hand'.

Discover your child's talents and abilities and help him/her to develop their potential in life.

'Dynamic Ageless You'.

A book about getting older without *ageing.* Combining Ancient Wisdom and modern Science, we now have the understanding, the information and the tools to live longer, fully functional lives.

CHANGE YOUR BELIEFS AND YOU CHANGE YOUR BIOLOGY!

Give yourself a FAITH-LIFT

'Angel Whispers'.

Short inspiring messages channelled from the Angels by Acushla (Anne   Hassett) With Angel Pictures contributed from her clients from around the world.

'Just for The Craic'.

A funny novel about Irish building workers in Swindon.

All of these books are available from Amazon.

C.D's.

DYNAMIC AGELESS YOU.

To help you to achieve an altered state of consciousness so that you may better re-programme your sub-conscious mind to change your biology, Anne has created a beautiful Self-Hypnosis C.D called Dynamic Ageless You.

ACUSHLAS ANGEL MEDITATION.

This very popular C.D was channelled to Anne/Acushla from the angels. It has four tracks.

Track   1. Chakra Clearing Meditation

2. Meet your Guardian Angel.

3. Receive healing from Archangel Raphael.

4. Time for yourself/ beautiful relaxing music.

You may listen to a 'taster' of this C.D on Anne's website.

www.acushlasangels.com

Printed in Great Britain
by Amazon.co.uk, Ltd.,
Marston Gate.